How Avoid Business Burnout

Small business guide

Alex Hall

© Alex Hall/ Alexandra Publications

All rights reserved world wide
No part of 'How to avoid Business Burnout' may be reproduced or stored by any means without the express permission of Alexandra Publications

Whilst reasonable care is taken to ensure the accuracy of the information in this publication, no responsibility can be accepted for the consequences of any actions based on any opinions, information or advice found in the publication.

Any Business information contained in this publication should not be taken as a substitute for professional advice. It is your own responsibility to comply with all legal, accounting and tax regulations. Please seek advice from your legal and accounting advisors. The author and publisher of this book used their best efforts in producing this book and disclaim liability arising directly or indirectly from the use of the information in this book.

ISBN-13: 978-1502944474

ISBN-10: 1502944472

Introduction 4
1 Choose the Right Business 8
2 Choose the Right Niche 14
3 Accumulate Knowledge 20
4 Create Systems 24
5 Don't Do Too Much! 29
6 Use Your Strengths 33
7 Learn to Specialise 37
8 Network in the Right Way 42
9 Plan to Succeed 46
Conclusion 51

Introduction

So many people dream for years of creating their own business.

It's their aim in life, escape the rat race, take control of their own destiny, be in charge of their own life and create time for their family.

For some it will remain an eternal pipe dream. They never find just the right time to make the break. Next year will always be a better time and the dream remains just that, a perfect daydream that will never have to face the trials of reality.

But many do take that amazing, exciting, terrifying step into the unknown, and for many, that's when the real trouble starts!

Don't get me wrong, I've been involved in running small businesses and mentoring those entering the business world for over thirty years – and I still love it.

It can be the most wonderful, exhilarating experience you will ever have.

You'll work hard – much harder than you would in a 9-5, but you'll know that you are creating your own kingdom – no matter how large or small that may be.

You can choose.

That's one of the biggest benefits, having control over the choices in your life.

You can choose what business you want to have. You can choose where you want to run it. You can make choices about what type of organization you want to spend your time on – a small business where everyone feels like family and many are family! Or you can be planting the seeds for an empire – every worldwide brand on the stock exchange had to start somewhere.

People want to start a business for many different reasons.

Some have a burning passion for a subject, whether that it creating wonderful wedding cakes, individual hand carved furniture, a completely new piece of technology or a new range of organic beauty products.

Some have always dreamt of escaping the rat race and living in the country running their own tea rooms or bed and breakfast. There are couples who have had enough of being ships in the night and want a chance to work together, and new mothers who need to be able to control their own hours and place of work.

Some professionals want to be in charge of their own destiny rather than dancing to someone else's tune, while others see a gap in the market and want to be the one to fill it.

But the fact is, that running your own business is hard work – especially in the first few years.

You are responsible for your own success and working a few days a week, having long lunches, driving a new expensive car and taking luxury holidays is not the way to find success.

Unfortunately I've seen a number of people who found that out the hard way and that's definitely not a pattern you want to follow.

There's always going to be some risk in starting your own business. There will always be days when you wonder why you left the safety of the 9-5, but this book is about something far more dangerous than that.

It's about Business Burnout.

Being tired, doubting yourself a little, working for long hours and certainly earning less than you could as an employee, those are the kind of things you will have to face in the early days of your enterprise, but they are just part of the process. If you have chosen the right path for you - you will take them in your stride – most of the time at least.

Having the odd day when you wonder what on earth you have done, is normal and you'll be feeling back on track again a day or two later. That's just part of the process.

Business Burnout is a different thing altogether.

Business Burnout can destroy your health as well as your fledgling business. It can damage your family life and your future prosperity. It can be devastating, and facing the danger is the best way to avoid it.

I've written this short book to show you the risk areas that every business faces, and once you know what the risks are, you can work to avoid them before they ruin your dreams.

Some of the decisions can be made when you're first planning your new enterprise. Others can be introduced into your business as time goes on and some can help you if you find that you feel you are heading towards business breakdown.

Remember, there's always an answer, even if it means a fresh start.

1 Choose the Right Business

One of the first decisions you make in the life of any business is - what business?

It sounds obvious and most of the time it is - you choose to start a business from something you love.

But.

The hobby that you love - whether that is baking party cakes, teaching members of your family how to drive, taking photographs, taking care of the accounts for your local club or church - might become something you hate the thought of if you have to do it day in, day out and find that your whole income depends on it.

Having to face something that you have come to hate, day after day is one of the fastest paths to Business Burnout that you could find.

It's far worse than having to go to a job you hate, because you can't cling onto the dream of leaving it all to start your own business.

You don't feel that you can just walk away once you've invested you're future in it. Although that is just what you might have to do if you find yourself in this position.

It's much better to make the decision yourself and cut your losses rather than keep on doing something you have learnt to hate, until you are forced out of it, either by a financial or health crisis.

The way to avoid this serious problem is to take some time to think very seriously, calmly and unemotionally before you take the steps to actually go into business.

Don't see a picture book tea shop when you're on holiday, discover it is for sale and rush in to purchase the whole business.

In fact you should never take an important financial decision when you're on holiday. You're brain is in 'holiday' mode, not 'real life' mode.

Many people have discovered this the hard way, either by deciding to move to the perfect holiday village or by investing in a business in that wonderful holiday spot.

So it's fine to have ideas, get inspiration, even to decide that it is time to make life changing decisions. A holiday is wonderful for that type of thinking. Your brain can take a rest from the day to day grind of work and you have the opportunity to think.

That's all wonderful. What isn't wonderful is rushing to see the estate agent or accountant and making a firm offer because 'it's a once in a lifetime chance and you have to decide now before it's too late and someone else gets in before you!'

Don't be pushed.

You know the saying "fools rush in where Angels fear to tread"! All too often it can be true and what looks likes a perfect, not to be missed opportunity, can turn into a nightmare. You must always take the time to think seriously – very seriously - about starting your own business.

Think long and hard before making your decision on any business idea, because a cute tea shop doesn't just involve the busy summer weekends with the shop full of customers. It also involves the wet winter Wednesdays when you don't see a customer all day.

It involves the food safety regulations, the baking and sourcing of all the products you will need.

It involves paperwork, tax returns, employment regulations and dealing with staff and all the potential problems that can bring with it.

It will involve early starts and late finishes, it will involve seven day weeks and probably no holidays for the first year or two while you get your business up and running.

If you love what you're doing this is all worthwhile, in fact it's all part of the excitement of creating your own business. But if you've chosen it on a whim because you like giving tea parties and think you'd be great at running a tea shop - you could be on the fast track to Business Burnout.

It doesn't mean that you're a failure in business, it just means you've chosen the wrong business for you.

If you end up dreading the thought of going to work in the morning, you need to make some changes – fast.

The planning part of your fledgling business is a very important part and you should not skimp on it. It can be very tempting when you're desperate to leave a job you hate, but planning will make all the difference to your success.

Of course, that doesn't mean that you should spend so much time planning that you never actually make the move - that's not planning, that's daydreaming.

So, plan realistically.

If it is possible, try to gather some experience in your chosen field, especially if it's a complete change of direction for you.

Some businesses lend themselves to being started on a part time basis. You can take on some of the work at weekends while you keep the day job.

Okay, it means that you end up working 7 days a week for a while, which is bound to be tiring. But the excitement of creating your own business can carry you through that for a while and it's an ideal way to discover what the business actually involves rather than just what you imagine it will involve.

It also means that you will be able to experience the full package of running a business.

It's so much more than turning up to do the fun bit. You have to find your customers, find your suppliers, learn the legal requirements, keep accurate accounts and accurate records, fill in tax returns and a host of other things that you might not have thought of.

The benefit of a 'try out' period is that you can actually find out if you enjoy the business you thought you'd love.

Deciding to close down a part time business is so much easier while you still have the safety net of your full time job.

When you have reached to point of deciding that you do want to start your own business, do some serious research so that you know what it will entail.

If you've never been involved in the running of a business you should do some research into the legal and tax obligations.

There are many books, websites and organisations that you will find helpful at this stage and they will help you can find guidance on what running a business actually entails. Many of the banks will also have literature on the basics that you might not have thought of.

Business tax, personal tax, business insurance, health insurance, account keeping, advertising, trade bodies, local regulations and restrictions, finding funding and grants – the list can seem endless when you first start thinking about it. But don't let it put you off, you just need to know about them so that you can set your business up properly.

Then think seriously about the business you are considering.

And at this stage I do mean think seriously.

It's all very well to love fixing computers for your friends and family in your spare time. You might find that it helps you relax and wind down from your daily work. But can you actually see yourself doing it full time? And how will you feel if you have to deal with customer expectations rather than having to just tell a friend that you can't fix the problem.

If you can see yourself doing that – and it still feels like a wonderful plan – great, you have the makings of a successful and personally fulfilling business.

If you can't – you'll be heading for Business Burnout.

So step back. Think seriously so that you can see your plan clearly rather than through rose coloured spectacles.

Once you've considered the picture clearly and logically, then go ahead.

You might decide to fine tune some of your original ideas. For instance you might decide that the idea of sharing your home all the time with complete strangers in a bed and breakfast isn't actually as appealing when you think seriously about it and you might decide to buy a property that you can develop as self catering apartments instead.

And on closer inspection the idea of a tea shop might lose some of its appeal but an outside catering business might be a much better idea for you.

Think carefully, chose wisely and avoid Business Burnout.

2 Choose the Right Niche.

Any industry can be seen as a broad brush and finding the right niche for you in that industry is vital to creating a successful business and avoiding Business Burnout.

According to the Oxford Dictionary, a niche is:

"A comfortable or suitable position in life or employment" for instance, *"he is now head chef at a leading law firm and feels he has found his niche"*

When you are beginning out in your new business you must realise that you cannot possible be all things to all people.

You will have to choose an area that you will specialise in.

If you're a baker you really can't compete with the large supermarkets by producing basic bread. They will always be able to sell for less than you can. So unless you are opening in a town that doesn't have easy access to a large supermarket, you will have to specialise and offer something different. That might be artisan bread, special cakes, gluten free products or focusing on recipes from a specific country.

Finding the right niche for your business will make all the difference to your happiness and to avoiding Business Burnout.

It's the difference between constantly struggling to compete in a crowded market and just making ends meet, and becoming a specialist in your own lucrative field.

And this is true for any area of business.

For this example we'll consider photography and think of the number of niches that there are in this one industry.

Many people love photography and dream of becoming a professional and spending their days doing what they enjoy. Of course, we've already tackled that running a business involves of lot more than that.

But let us just stay with photography for the moment.

Normally the first area that springs to mind when someone thinks of turning their photography hobby into a business is the wedding market.

And why not?

There are hundreds of weddings taking place almost every weekend in every part of the country.

You might even have done the semi official photos for the wedding of a friend or relative and had rave reviews from them.

So, it's a big market and you've had some experience, naturally you'll choose to be a wedding photographer.

But there's a huge difference between taking the photos for a friend and creating a perfect album for a demanding bride – and let's face it, not every bride and groom are going to be perfectly photogenic!

Being a professional wedding photographer can be a very exciting, a very satisfying but also a very stressful profession and your own personal style has to suit your clients.

They probably don't want totally candid shots, a photojournalist record of their perfect day! They want a romantic, perfect photo album and there is always a lot of work in processing the images after the actual day, so wedding photography just doesn't suit every photographer.

There are many niches in the photography industry apart from weddings.

- Studio portraits
- School or corporate portraits
- Children's portraits
- Pet portraits
- Event photography
- Product photography
- Fine art
- Photojournalism
- Sport
- Food
- Landscape
- Nature & wildlife

- Fashion
- Advertising
- Travel
- Architecture
- Calendars & greeting cards
- Stock photography.

If you love working with people, you'll probably hate spending all your time focusing closely on flowers and plants for seed catalogues.

Equally, if you prefer being able to concentrate on the detail of your images and produce beautiful works of art, dealing with children for family portraits or having to produce hundreds or even thousands of standard and at times clichéd images for a stock library could soon lead to you hating your camera and to Business Burnout.

The very thing that had always been your escape, your freedom and your indulgence, can easily become the very thing that you find most stressful if you choose the wrong niche, even when you think you are choosing it for the right reasons.

The same can be said for almost any area of business, even when it seems to be quite straightforward.

If you're an accountant, do you want to spend your time working on the books of large companies or would you prefer to specialize in one area of industry and really be able to learn to understand their particular challenges, for instance farming, artisan food producers or our friend the photographer.

There are certain practical questions to face when entering any industry and choosing your niche.

You have to be aware of how much competition there is and if the market can really stand another player.

If you want to open that tea shop in a really busy tourist destination, the fact that there are already five tea shops in town might not be a problem – especially if you can add something different to make your tea shop stand out. But if there are five tea and coffee shops in a local shopping street, there could be absolutely nothing you can do to make enough people choose your tea shop on a regular basis. And before you think it, just trying to be the cheapest is never a good business model for a small business.

You also have to take account of the general range of prices charged in that niche.

Again, you shouldn't simply aim to undercut the lowest prices, that road will lead straight to bankruptcy. You might get lots of orders – although not necessarily, sometimes being the cheapest just makes potential customers think that your service or product will be substandard.

But even if you do manage to find lots of orders, that will be absolutely no good if you don't make any profit on all that work.

So, make some sound business enquiries and work out if there is a market for your idea and how much you will be able to charge, but don't just use that to make your decision and end up trying to create your new business in an area you hate.

The best reason for going into business and creating a successful, long term business is to choose something you love doing. Then the tough times – and there will be tough times – will be something you can get through rather than a swift road to Business Burnout.

The best thing in the world is earning your living while doing something you love. When you're doing that, you're never really working!

3 Accumulate Knowledge

Almost anyone who is new to running a business will discover quite quickly that they don't know as much as they thought they did.

Even if you have worked in the industry for a number of years there will be areas that you have never even considered before you find yourself running your own business.

You might have been driving delivery vans for many years but have you ever really thought about how to arrange the servicing schedule, negotiate contracts, combine a number of different part loads or fill in the tax returns.

Any industry that looks easy from the outside, or even close to the inside, actually involves a lot more than might seem at first.

You might be a brilliant designer of wedding dresses, and your sewing skills might be second to none. But when you decide to set up on your own, creating beautiful one-off designer wedding dresses you will also need to know a lot more about a lot more subjects.

You will have to know how to price them so that you will make a profit but still be able to compete in your market.

You will have to know where to find a photographer who can capture the beauty of your designs and make them attractive to a bride.

You will have to know how to set up a website and link it with the world so that the world can find you.

You will have to be able to deal with customers and make sure that they actually pay you for your work. You will have to have the confidence to require a significant deposit if you are creating a unique dress, and to have a contract that sets out what you will supply so that everyone knows exactly what is expected before you start on the dress.

You will have to find suppliers, not just for fabrics but boxes, dress bags, hangers and dress rails, maybe extras such as shoes, jewellery and tiaras as well as all the other business requirements.

You will have to be able to keep records, send out invoices, arranging printing and advertising, press releases and displays at wedding fairs.

It can be overwhelming and frustrating when you know there's always more that you need to learn and it can become extremely stressful if you let it overpower you.

But learning is part of the process and it can be a very enjoyable part.

Most industries have associations, magazines, websites and trade bodies and they are a great source of information, contacts and advice.

There are many, many business books available that will guide you through the basic requirements of setting up a business, and most of the banks also produce very helpful literature.

You can also find a lot of information on the internet. In the UK the website www.gov.uk will provide a lot of very helpful and clear information, while in the USA www.sba.gov is an official website of the United States government.

Don't feel that you have to learn everything at once. Of course there are things you will have to be aware of from the very beginning, especially any legal requirements for your business such as specific health and safety regulations for toy making or working in the food industry for instance.

But it's also possible to allow yourself to become swamped with the need to know more, gain more knowledge, to invest in the next business book or piece of magic computer software.

Don't allow yourself to be swamped by the minutiae, the small and often trivial details of a process. Perfectionism is wonderful to a point, but there can come a stage when it simply overwhelms you and stops you functioning altogether. In other words - Business Burnout.

If you find yourself facing a problem you really don't have the knowledge to deal with, bring in an expert. You don't actually have to employ a marketing director or webmaster, you can invest in some time with a consultant or work in a local business group, possibly exchanging some of your specialist knowledge with someone who knows what you don't.

A photographer who's organising a lavish anniversary party might be more than willing to give some help and advice to someone who creates wonderful party cakes.

If you need more knowledge personally, find a book or a local education course. If you need knowledge you don't have, find someone who does.

Spend some money on solving the problems and spend your time on earning the money doing what you are good at.

Over time you will widen your own skill set and you will also become more comfortable at working with other professionals when you need their skills.

As your business grows you will be able to afford to bring in other people with different skills to you own so that you can concentrate on your own strengths, and of course they are the very thing that brought you into your business in the first place.

You will have to learn to build your business around you rather than allowing it to become the master.

You want to flourish alongside your business, not be dragged down into Business Burnout.

4 Create Systems

Being organised is wonderful in every branch of life, but it makes a huge difference when you're running a business.

One of the biggest reasons for the kind of overwhelming stress that leads to Business Burnout is being disorganised.

The difference between a stress free organisation and chaos -is a set of good systems.

The word system can be used to mean many different things, but it certainly doesn't have to mean some extremely expensive, complex computer programme. In fact they can cause you even more trouble if the 'system' is too complicated and over detailed for your needs. You might never be able to completely understand it and get the best use out of it. It can end up being the source of your stress and Business Burnout.

In fact, I know of one company where they are paying hundreds of pounds every week for a system that creates more problems than it solves and they spend hours every week correcting the mistakes it creates! Definitely a probable cause for Business Burnout.

So what sort of systems do you need?

Some way of keeping track of everything and making the running of your business more efficient.

You don't need anything to add to the stress of running your business.

Write a list of all the things you have to do on a regular basis.

- Sending out invoices
- Sending out quotations
- Preparing contracts
- Recording outgoings
- Paying regular bills
- Updating a website
- Sending out orders
- Ordering stock
- Keeping a record of stock levels
- Making new contacts
- Checking the bank statements
- Competing tax returns

Some things are required in every type of business such as the financial aspects of running a business, while others vary from industry to industry.

But the only way to keep on top of everything is to have a system, otherwise you will end up completing your quarterly tax return at the very last minute every time, being stressed about it and staying up late the night before you have to submit it.

It will be the reason for your worry, anxiety, sleepless nights and you'll probably make errors which will cause you even more worry – a sure way to Business Burnout if you follow that pattern across many of the regular tasks that have to be done.

Although it might sound very boring and pedestrian, the only way to avoid this terror inducing mess is to have a system in place.

The system has to suit you and it has to allow some flexibility – but it has to be there.

The other main reason to have a business system is to automate as much as the process as possible so that someone else can take it on as the business grows and you employ more people.

If the system is efficient you can train someone else to do it, so that the business can run without your constant presence. Being indispensible isn't actually a good thing – it means you can never take time off.

Creating a habit of creating systems is the best way to start this.

At first they can be quite simple. A schedule for sending out emails, a time of the day or week for sending out the invoices – each type of business will have a different pattern.

Write down a list of the regular things that your business requires.

If your customer orders arrive online – set a time each day to process them and a cut off time for dispatch.

If you keep checking your emails every ten minutes and rushing off to pack up the latest order, you will be completely tied to that task and all the rest of the tasks that have to be done will be pushed into corners to be rushed and done without proper thought but lots of stress.

So create your list of tasks, set a schedule for completing these tasks and create a routine.

You can have daily, weekly and even monthly or quarterly routines for certain tasks. But having that schedule – and it is always better if you write it down – will help you create a routine so that you will be freed from the constant worry and stress of unnecessary deadlines.

You can also create templates for the documents that you have to send out regularly. So when you have to send a quotation, the basis of the letter and contract is already on the computer and you will just have to fill in the necessary details rather than start with a blank screen.

Making things as simple as possible ensures that the tasks are actually completed.

A mailing list that is easy to print out as a set of labels will mean that you actually send out your advertising on a regular schedule rather than constantly putting it off because you can't face typing out the addresses. The time invested in creating the system will save you far more hours that it takes to create in the first place and it will remove the stress in the future.

As your business grows you will find you have to add more systems. Systems for staff rotas, staff holidays, training, recruiting, interviewing, and creating staff contracts.

You might need to complete tender documents for larger contracts, and having a system that deals with that means that you will actually complete them rather than finding that an important document is due in the next day and you haven't even started to look at the details

When you start your business with systems and routines, you will naturally develop the systems and methods to suit your business growth and you will be able to avoid the stress of disorder and chaos that can lead so quickly to Business Burnout.

It also means that your business will have the framework that it needs to grow and develop into a larger organisation and the systems that will allow other people to take many of the regular tasks away from your own desk, giving you time and the space to concentrate on the future of your business.

5 Don't Do Too Much!

This can be a serious problem when you start a business but it can lead to Business Burnout very quickly.

There are certainly a lot of things that do need to be done in the start up and early stages of a business and the adrenalin and excitement will keep you going through this.

In fact, working sixteen hours a day while you first get up and running can be exciting. Who wants to waste time at the cinema when you could be painting your new shop, putting the finishing touches to your first collection or creating your new recipes?

But this only works for the very first stages of a business, it can easily become a habit and it will lead to Business Burnout very quickly.

When your business is new, you will have to take on most of the tasks yourself. After all, you won't have the resources to outsource lots of tasks or to employ many people, especially for the daily tasks.

But you have to realise that you can't do everything. It's far better to do fewer things well and give your business a strong base from which to grow.

So, prioritise the tasks and focus on the ones that bring in the best results.

As an example, if you design wedding jewellery you will probably want to have a presence on social media – many types of business across many industries find that social media is an important part of their marketing mix.

But it's vital to expend your energy on the parts that actually work for you, and the truth is that a lot of social media presence and advertising doesn't actually achieve much.

Facebook might be the site that most people think of first, but if you are selling to a specific market – such as brides to be –you'd probably be much better off creating a strong presence on a specialist site for weddings, or the type of social media that attracts your target audience.

Facebook and Twitter might have lots of followers for you, but are all these hundreds or thousands of followers leading to any sales?

The quality of the results is the only thing that matters in business, not the boost to your ego of lots of empty attention.

The same process can be followed for any type of business.

If you sell handmade jams and chutneys at farmer's fairs, take the time to actually look at the results. You might 'take' more money at a large event, but do you actually 'make' more money?

Once you take into account the time, the rent and the travelling costs, you might actually clear more money by going to smaller more local events.

Of course if you also offer a mail order service through your website, you will have to take into account the value of the orders generated from different events.

Sticking with the idea of jams and chutneys – don't try to create every single recipe that you have. It is far better to focus your energy on a core selection at first and make them as well as you can, create a good reputation and then grow from there.

Whatever part of your business you look it, it is possible to try to do too much, and very tempting to think that you have to be able to do everything in your plan from the very first day, but this is a sure and fast way to Business Burnout.

The stress of trying to do everything at once will lead to failure – no one can do everything. No business can be all things to all people, and no one in the world can run a large corporation on their own!

You have to focus on what absolutely has to be done and do those tasks quickly and efficiently.

Don't put them off while you check your emails or Facebook pages.

Tick them off your list and remove the stress of having them always on your mind. Things that have to be done will grow into monsters in your mind if you leave them.

Running a business is about balance. You will have to juggle a lot of things, so you don't want to waste your time on tasks that don't matter and don't bring in results.

Cut out the tasks that don't bring positive returns and you'll free up time to concentrate on those that do, and to do them better and avoid Business Burnout.

As your business grows you will be able to employ more people and outsource more tasks, and then you will be able to concentrate on your own personal strengths, which are of course the reason you started the business in the first place.

Doing what you love is always the best way to avoid Business Burnout.

6 Use Your Strengths

Everyone has strengths and weakness – knowing what they are and being honest with yourself is much more important that you may think.

There's a tendency to think that you have to be able to do it all yourself, but no one can be good at everything.

And the fact is, if you continually concentrate on tasks that you are not good at, you will not only waste a lot of time, it will drain you of your mental energy and your will to continue, and it will quickly lead to Business Burnout.

If you feel that your business must have a website to succeed, but you don't know the first thing about building a successful website or designing something attractive – don't do it.

If you are interested in becoming a web designer, by all means find a course and teach yourself the skills you want, but not at the cost of your business.

Any time spent focusing on something that is unnecessary is taking time directly away from your road to success.

So either find a web company that has a good selection of easy to use on-line templates, and then you can simply add your own company information to the template you choose, or find someone else who can do your website for you.

Of course, you should take a long hard look at whether you really do need a website at all in the early stages of your business. Don't allow yourself to get carried away on someone else's idea. After all, do you need a worldwide presence for your local car repair shop?

You have to realise that it's far too easy to waste hours on a task that someone else could do in minutes.

Take the time – this is time well spent, not wasted – to really decide what your strengths are.

If you are looking at a cake business, are your real strengths in the baking or the design and decorating of cakes. If you excel at creating wonderful, imaginative and beautifully decorated cakes, it might be worth paying someone else to actually bake the cakes so that you can concentrate on the design side of the business. After all, it's the design that makes them different and allows you to charge more than you could for an ordinary Victoria sponge.

If your strength is in writing a book, don't spoil your chances of success by insisting on doing your own cover if design is not your area. Invest in a cover that will sell your book and give you a better chance of success.

If you feel that your wedding jewellery design business has to have a strong presence on social media but you don't know where to start, find someone who can do that side of things for you, or at least find someone who can teach you rather than wasting hours, days or even weeks trying to work your way through the jungle.

Spending time trying to do something that is not your strength can suck the energy right out of you and can lead to you loosing the interest in your new business altogether.

It can make everything a chore that has to be struggled through.

The areas where you have a problem will loom larger and larger in your life, dominating all your time and keeping you awake at night as you worry about them.

At the same time, the parts of the business that you love and that drew you into creating your own business in the first place, will lose their attraction as you rush through them to get back to the bits that you struggle with, and frankly hate.

So why does this lead to burnout? Because you're focusing on things you're not good at and concentrating on tasks you are learning to hate.

It will drain your energy, you will spend hours doing things that shouldn't be taking your time and you will learn to hate the business altogether.

It's a fast track to Business Burnout.

So write down your strengths and weakness, farm out the weaknesses to someone who's good at them and concentrate your energy on your strengths.

Remember – it makes a lot more sense to work to your strengths than spending all your energy working on your weaknesses!

7 Learn to Specialise

This is similar to working on your strengths, and again you need to sit down and work out what exactly your strengths are.

But in this case you are focusing on the exact area of your strength in the business you are already in or are thinking of entering.

It goes along with finding your niche.

As a small business you cannot possibly be all things to all people. Even if you could attract all the possible customers in your area, you couldn't fulfil all the orders.

So doesn't it make more sense to focus on what you're really good at and set out to be the best fish in a small pond rather than just getting lost in a big lake?

Focusing all your energy on trying to be everything to everyone will mean that you are jumping from project to project, never really succeeding as well as you could in any of them, and getting seriously stressed. This is another fast track to Business Burnout.

People often see multi-tasking as a good thing.

But in fact you are likely to achieve far more if you actually focus all your attention on one thing at a time. Complete that task and then move onto the next one. You are likely to get though the work faster and - even more importantly - more accurately with fewer mistakes.

There's nothing more time wasting and more likely to sap your energy than having to repeat the same work over and over again before you actually get it right.

When you focus your whole business attention on a niche, when you specialise in what you are really good at and on the part of the industry that you actually enjoy, you will be able to concentrate your attention and the attention of your business much more effectively.

Take a step back from the day to day running of your business and think clearly and unemotionally about what you actually do.

- What services or products do you offer?
- Which area do you enjoy the most?
- Where do you have less competition?
- Where do you make the best profits?
- Where do you make the most money?

Turnover and profit are not the same thing, although far too many people in business get them mixed up.

You can turn over a hundred thousand and make a comfortable profit.

You can turn over a million and lose money.

Then there are other questions. What are your aims in running your business?

Do you want to create something that you can enjoy and make a comfortable living from?

Do you want to create a business that will grow and expand into a business empire and float on the stock market? Every multinational company started somewhere.

Do you want to create something in between, that you and your family can treasure, work in and that you will pass onto the next generation?

Do you want to create a successful start up that you can sell to a larger company in a few years, allowing you to take the profits and start another business? Some entrepreneurs enjoy the start up and creation of a business but don't enjoy the day to day running of an established company.

None of these things are right or wrong, they're just different.

Once you have a clearer idea of exactly what you are aiming for you have a better chance of succeeding. After all, if you don't set goals it's very difficult to decide when you're reached them!

So, decide what you want. Decide what area of your industry you should specialise in.

Where is there a gap in the market? It's always much easier to sell against fewer competitors. Just make sure that there is actually a market in that gap.

A small business has some strengths that a large organisation can't even dream of.

You can see an opportunity and jump at it. You don't need to hold meetings, order reports, approach your directors and wait months for the supply chain to be implemented. You can see an opportunity, design your product or service and have it in the marketplace quickly.

Where are the best profit margins?

It's all very well making 1p on each item if you can sell millions, but if you can only sell a few thousand or a few hundred you need a much better profit margin. If you specialise and offer a specialist service or product, you can charge a premium.

If you're a baker, what's the point of trying to compete on price with the big superstore? If you specialise in artisan bread and luxury bakes you can charge more. After all, there's a limit to how much you can actually make, so concentrate on the smaller more profitable part of the market rather than wasting your time and energy trying to fill the bottom of the market, especially when it's already full of other companies.

Trying to be all things to all people will fail. Even the big companies don't try to do that. They focus on their target market.

So decide on your target market and specialise in that.

For a small business, the decision to specialise is all important. It can be the difference between failure and stunning success.

Specialise personally – making the most of your strengths within your business.

Specialise in your product or service, find you niche in the market and become the name to go to rather than just one of hundreds of companies with the same offering.

Specialise, create a name, become the expert. Make your company the name that springs to mind when someone wants the service that you offer. Many of the biggest companies grew by being a specialist at first. Some large cosmetic companies had a single ground breaking product.

'Don't ask the price, it's a penny' was the slogan for Marks and Spencer's first bazaar in Leeds and when the company began to grow it was based on the five key principals of Quality, Value, Service, Innovation and Trust and even after more than 120 years, they still have a clear idea of where they specialise – even if it is quite a large area!

So learn to focus your energy on your strengths – both your own personal energy and strengths and those of your growing business.

8 Network in the Right Way

The whole concept of networking can be difficult to balance when you go into business.

After all, what is networking?

It means creating connections between you and other people, between your business and other businesses.

But it can be hard to find the balance between working and networking.

You have to spend time on building your own business, but you also need to step back from it to be able to see the bigger picture.

You can network locally with local businesses.

You can network with other companies in your own industry.

You can network with people who have some common link such as a business woman's network or a young entrepreneur's network.

With the internet you can now network nationally or even globally.

Networks bring people with some common interest together so that everyone can benefit - in theory.

But networking can also be a very good way of distracting your attention and wasting your time.

Starting your own business can and will be very time consuming and stressful.

You are stepping into a completely new world and it doesn't take very long to discover that you don't know everything you thought you did. Indeed that there were things you didn't even know you should know!

Even someone with a degree in Business Management can get quite a shock when they actually start to run a business.

If you join up with the right business network you will be able to get to know other people who either have the same problems - making you feel better about not knowing - or who have a different skill set to you so that you can all share and work together.

You can form links where you can share your areas of expertise and help each other to grow your businesses.

So you need to network to get to know other people in your field, as well as to find possible clients and partners.

But if you spend too much time networking you might not be leaving yourself enough time to actually work on your business.

To network or not to network – that is the question!

If you spend too much time trying to work and not enough time talking to other business owners, mentors or people who are trying to start their own business, you can suffer from Business Burnout because you feel as if you're all alone on your journey.

Learning that there are other people who have been in exactly the same position as you can help rebuild your confidence when you're feeling overwhelmed. Especially when you feel that you've bitten off more than you can chew.

Spending time with other people who know what you are going through can boost your confidence and energy when you are suffering a bad patch. Of course, you don't want to pour out all your woes, networking is about being positive and making connections, it isn't a session with your psychiatrist!

The opposite of not networking enough is networking too much.

This can lead you to comparing your level of success to others that you see as more successful than you.

Of course, they might just be better at portraying an aura of success or they might have just been in business a lot longer than you have.

There's a fine balance between being inspired by others, so that you take action to create your own success, and simply watching their success until it brings you down.

If you spend week after week listening to their tales of success, it will sap your energy and it can leave you feeling uninspired and dejected.

However, you do still need to take some breaks from work and meeting with other like minded people can be a great help. You can swap ideas, swap skills, find new business or learn about promotional techniques that have worked for them.

Some types of networking will actually create orders for your company while you are finding the suppliers you need as well. Working together and creating business for each other is one of the main aims of many business groups.

So you have to find your own personal balance between spending all your time with your head down focusing on the day to day details of your business, and spending too much time – wasting time – networking with no measurable purpose other than socialising.

Creating balance in business and in your own work/life equation is one of the secrets for avoiding Business Burnout.

9 Plan to Succeed

It's all too easy to jump headlong into what you think will be a perfect business, an idea that will lead to almost instant success.

But there's a common phrase – a cliché if you like - that states:

People don't plan to fail, they fail to plan

It might seem boring, uninspired and time wasting, but if you don't spend some time planning you will end up simply wasting time, going in circles, rushing from task to task and not actually getting anywhere.

There are all types of planning that you really need to implement to make your business a success and help you avoid burnout.

There are different types of business planning.

Of course there is the overall plan, the business plan that you will take to bank managers and investors. The plan that lays out what your business will be, where the growth will come from, what the figures for income and outgoings will be, when you will break into profit and how much profit that will be.

These are very useful documents.

Apart from the fact that you will need a good business plan if you want anyone to lend you money, they are also a wonderful way of making you actually focus on what you expect your business to be in the next year, three years or five years. It can bring a bit of a reality check to your dreams because you have to actually think about where the money will be coming from and how much it will actually cost you to run and then grow the business.

You might also want to have an exit plan if you are a start-up entrepreneur.

There are many people who are strong in the area of starting a business and getting it up and running, but their strength doesn't lie in actually running an established business, and there's absolutely nothing wrong with this. You have to understand your own strengths and weaknesses.

If you are a start-up expert, then you need to have an exit strategy in place right at the beginning. A plan of what you want to do, the point you want to reach and how you will then exit and recover your investment.

Then there is the more mundane, but very important type of planning. How you actually get the work done.

If you make making weekly and monthly plans, you will avoid the common problem than many people running a small business end up with. That is that they end up wasting time each day trying to work out what they should do next and ending up with many tasks half done, but none completed.

This will quickly lead to frustration, little or no progress, and a failing business.

This works alongside having systems in your business. You must have systems, but you also need a timetable so that you know when you should work on which system.

Set up a timetable for yourself so that you know when you are going to focus on sending invoices, checking emails, making phone calls, working on the account system, doing tax returns and any of the other regular tasks that are required in your own business.

Once they have set times, you will know what you have to do and you'll avoid the problem of having a tax return that must be done but is left until the very last minute.

Dealing with constant deadlines and firefighting problems is never a comfortable or successful way to work.

You also have to spend time to plan your business growth.

Spend an hour or two at the beginning of each month deciding what you want to accomplish for the month, whether it's finding new clients, building your email list, working on tenders and contracts, making more sales or creating new products.

Define your monthly goals and then break those down into weekly tasks. One huge task can look impossible, but when you break it down into bite sized pieces it suddenly looks much more manageable.

Give yourself some time at the end of each day to review what tasks you have listed for the next day and set some time aside at the end or the beginning of the week to review your plan so that you enter the new week with a clear idea of what you intend to achieve and where you need to focus your attention.

Do the smaller piece each week and when you look back after a few months you'll be amazed at what you have achieved. You will also have trained yourself in new habits so that it's easy for you to continue with your new organised methods.

You should also look back at the end of each month and check what you have achieved out of your starting plan.

Some tasks will have to be allocated again for the next month, some will have to be done every month, and some goals won't be achieved in the time you set out. But you will have a clear picture of what you have achieved, what timescales you should set in future and you will be able to see the path you have actually followed rather than just fighting through an endless jungle with no clear path in sight.

That is so much more satisfying than looking back in six months and discovering that you still haven't got round to starting that new project that will make all the difference to your success.

Constantly failing to reach the targets you've set yourself and constantly trying to catch up with the small tasks that have grown into monsters, is a very good way of driving yourself to Business Burnout.

Although a plan is the best way to actually achieve your goals, whether that is weekly or annually, you do have to allow flexibility.

Don't fall into the trap of creating such a rigid plan that you can't adapt to an opportunity that presents itself. You should always allow for a chance opening that arrives out of the blue.

Your plans will grow, adapt to circumstances and allow you to change and move as you see how your business is developing, so don't be scared of altering your plans, even if it means going off in a direction you never even imagined.

Remember, flexibility is one of the biggest strengths of the small business and taking advantages of opportunities that present themselves is often the very thing that can change a business from just getting by into a success story.

So plan, but be prepared to adapt your plan.

Conclusion

Being in business is always a challenge, but it can be a wonderful challenge. Exciting, rewarding, fulfilling.

But of course it's also hard work and there will be times when you wonder what on earth you have done! Everyone feels like that at some point.

It's also very easy to fall into the habit of working 24/7, trying to do everything yourself, trying to take on too much before you've given the business a chance to develop, and being led by the advice of others rather than listening to your own opinions.

Building a business is hard work and it will take time.

But don't let yourself get discouraged or feel overwhelmed if things aren't working as fast as you'd like.

Just step back, look clearly at where the business is, where you want it to be, and which unimportant tasks you can eliminate to allow you time to focus on what's important.

This will stop you feeling overwhelmed and will allow you to see the bigger picture again.

Remember, everyone can feel overwhelmed at times – that's what holidays are for.

So learn to recognise the signs early and allow yourself the space and time to step back and re-evaluate.

Business Burnout isn't inevitable, but it is always a risk if you don't see the signs and give yourself the space to recover.

Never fall into the trap of feeling that you can't afford to take time out.

It's much easier to take a few days or even a couple of weeks than end up seriously ill, unable to think and totally burnt out. That won't do your business, your family or you any good at all.

So remember, if you feel that you are reaching the stage of suffering from Business Burnout, step back.

Better still, don't allow the stress to grow too serious in the first place. Stress is ok, some people need it, it keeps you fired up, and there is a type of good stress in dealing with mental challenges or emotional elation. These things might cause you stress, but it's good stress and will help you grow and learn.

But when stress begins to make you ill, keeps you awake at night, gives you constant headaches, makes you feel as if nothing is going right and makes you feel you are a failure – that's more than healthy stress, that's Business Burnout and you don't want to allow yourself to reach that stage.

So remember, if you are beginning to feel overwhelmed and overstressed, it's fine to take some time out and allow yourself to recover and see things clearly again.

It will give you the chance to get things back on the right track, recover some of your energy and enthusiasm and if necessary, rebuild your health.

Things *will* get better!

Enjoy your business.

Printed in Great Britain
by Amazon